A BELL BURIED DEEP

A BELL BURIED DEEP

VERONICA GOLOS

STORY LINE PRESS
2004

First Printing

Published by Story Line Press, Three Oaks Farm, PO Box 1240, Ashland, OR 97520-0055, www.storylinepress.com.

This publication was made possible thanks in part to the generous support of the Nicholas Roerich Museum and our individual contributors.

Interior design by Sara Glover
Author photo by Preston Merchant
Cover design by Sharon McCann
Cover art by Roberta Baskin Shefrin: *"Woman" is the dominant theme of my work. I am drawn to her soul and spirit – as distinguished from her body. My women are somewhat bound, forcing the energy from within – creating a mystery and melancholy bordering on the edge of sadness.*

Library of Congress Cataloging-in-Publication Data

Golos, Veronica
A bell buried deep / Veronica Golos.
p. cm.
ISBN 1-58654-031-9
1. Sarah (Biblical matriarch)—Poetry. 2. Hagar (Biblical figure)—Poetry. 3. Women—Poetry. I. Title. 4. Slavery—U.S.
PS3607.O487 B45 2003
811'.6—dc21

2003011251

For David, who is love

TABLE OF CONTENTS

CREATION

GENESIS

➤

EXODUS

CODA

A BELL BURIED DEEP

Feasting on the aftertaste,
I weaken first,
rise, stand at the window –
my pale skin flushed in the North Carolina light.
The old wood planks moan,
the white bedspread ripples like new snow,
our white sheets are the color of white beneath white –
and you, your brown skin against the sheet,
our marriage the color of syrup.

I lift my eyes and am chastened
by the angry heartbreak this world can bring.
The treetops are tender green –
and what is the color green but everything
        washed clean,
even the tiny, blue stone cemetery
where my son remains...
does not rise even after this, his eleventh year.
He is blue in the ground, his light-blue bones,
the midnight cap of his hair, his infant smell –
a bell buried deep, where he was in me,
ringing, ringing.

My god,
love making
can redeem
but does not release
pain! I do not forget

➤

my periwinkle boy, my blue berry, my demon –
all his names in a world pulsing with names,
wild christenings in the air –
as the blue-green vein of my wrist beats,
the memory of him, our pale-boned boy,
drives me back to our bed
to touch you, his dark father,
with my grief full of tongues,
full with his name.

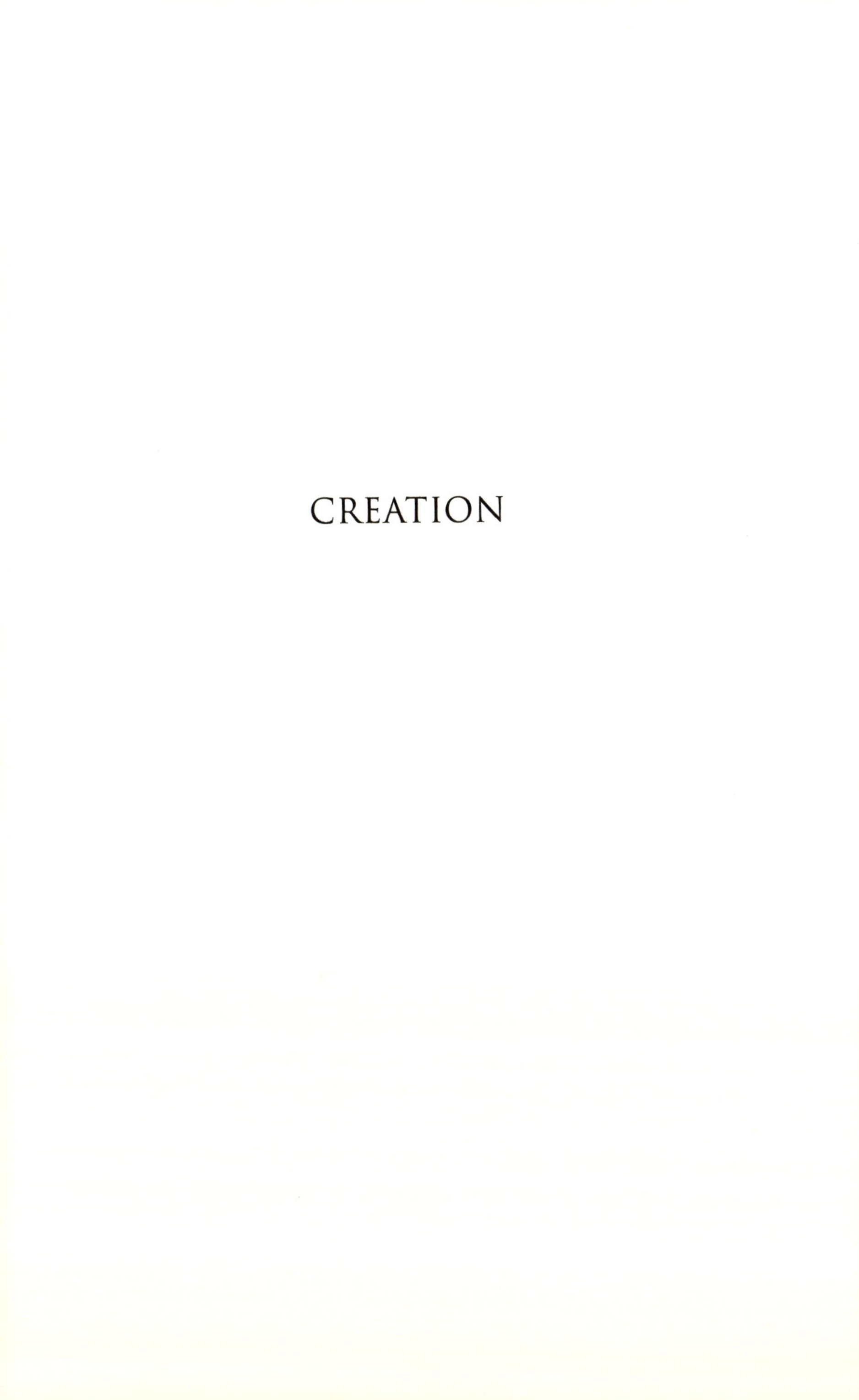

CREATION

THE KORÉ

I was stirred by touch.
Feeling spun me on my way.
I tapped a crazy cadence
And starlight gyrated,
Climaxed, each throb immense,
Till a sun was born that could feed
The void.

Looking down, there, pulsing
In the glitter – the bowl of earth.
Parts of sea and space leapt
From molecule to molecule – but
I prepared nothing; the wind blew hot,
And in the steam,
The wild and the bright met
And chaos congealed.

My name is written in the sperm
My secret's in the egg.
A billion years I brewed,
Cradled by the moon.
Resplendent, I replicated, split,
Fused, caused combustion and
Commotion, till, glutted with stars,
I was reborn,
A soaking muddy beast, reeking
And alone.

MAMI WATA

On pilings green with moss, we sit, listening
to the sea's hiss and come, its pause –
purple shadows flying into the curves of sand.

Late in the day, a half moon hints in the sky. The sea
is not
blue, nor is it green, but a gray filled with blue
and green –
like a singer whose voice trembles at a note,
then overflows.

We have lived far from the ocean,
far from the cries and shapes of men,
their wild hearts tamed to the size of a thumb.

Even the gulls forget their sense of sea; they pick
and quarrel on land for bits of bread.

How good then to feel *Mami Wata*,
rolling and pulling; breathing her wet breath
beneath this sand – this *uwa mmadu* – this
human world.

THE MOTHER

My mother has gone quiet – a silence not of lack,
        or fear
or anger, but of a great attention – a leaning into.

She has left the language of populations,
consequence, variety – even the clamor

of need, she forgets. She smiles at the back and forth
of talk; the *art* of give and take.

She hears what's underneath.
Child, she whispers, *the sun splashes into the sea;*
when the clouds shift, their touch
against the sky rustles
like silk touching thigh.

She is leaving this world.
Her listening is a kind of touch,

the way you'd feel along a wall – intent,
imagining.

She fills and is filled – is glass, pitcher,
water flowing. She stands at the center

of endless concentric circles, at the navel
of the world, from which infinite lines emerge –

a hand through water,
making ripples...

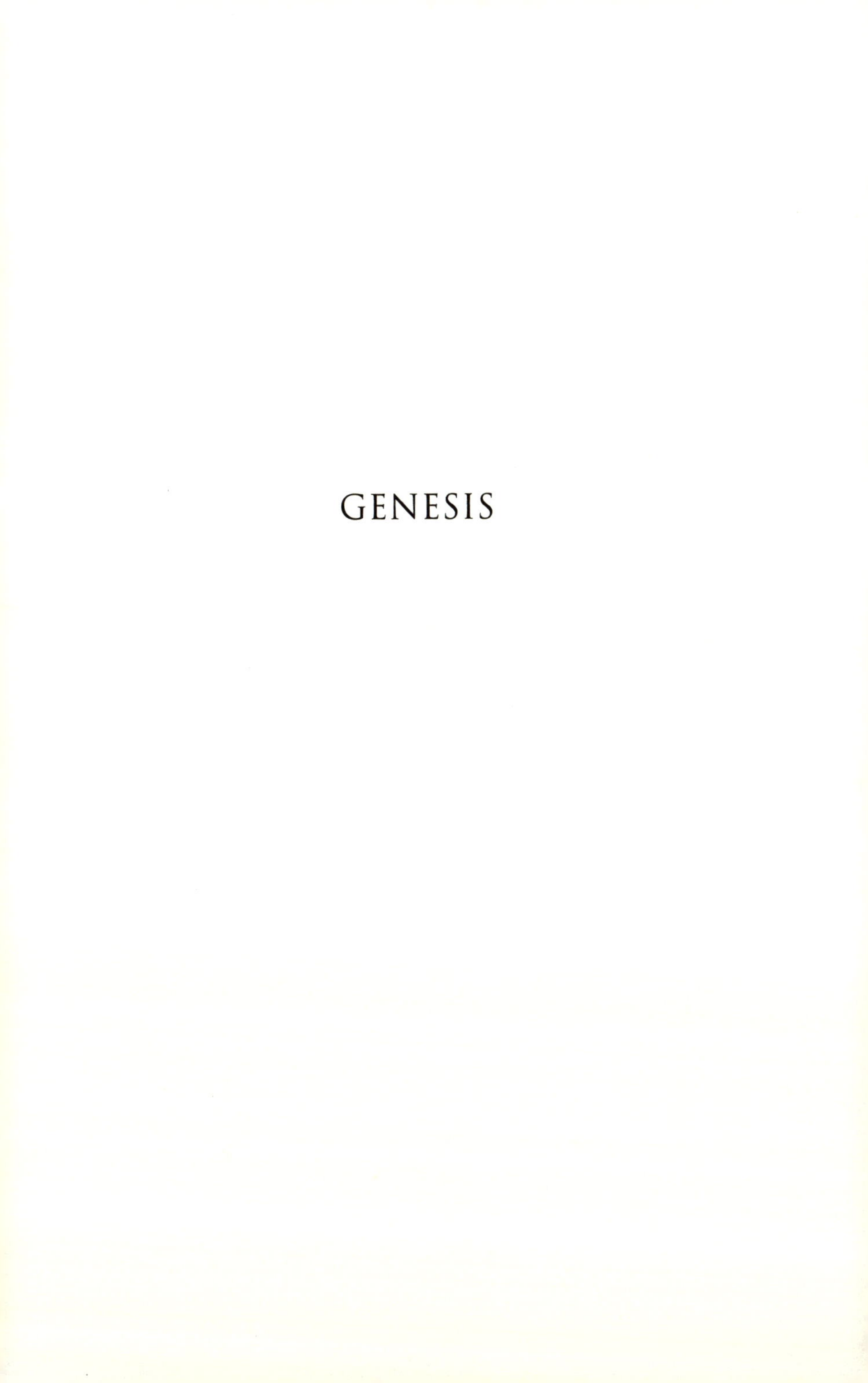

GENESIS

THE CASTING OF STONES

She is raw, as if a great hand whittled her down
    to bone.
She gleams beneath her eyes; she is full with the death
    of desire,
with the absence of useless moons. She is the
    conundrum
of what is filled, her emptiness beyond our ken;
    she holds
nothing; her skin, a sieve. She is gone beyond
us, where dust is water and water, sprinkling sand.
We have walked with our sandals upon her; we
    have leaned
into her void. We have called out her name
in the desert; we have found twelve polished stones.

MIDDLE PASSAGE

I

Do the dead leave a trail,
Fumes and moist places,
Stay – even when we will them away?
If we speak – and they answer,
Are their words a tangible proof of love?

What's speaking here
If not the rounding of spirit;
The dead come to breath in our mouth?

II

I bare my dreams beneath the gristle of my back.
Those long ago roads; all taken.

Can I offer what I no longer have?
Or does the offer itself, reclaim?

What's this beneath my thumb? A blade of
Grass – thrumming; its small root

A drum. Was I meant to come
Into the world broken? I almost understand this

Seeming – just there – just here –
Before me.

GOING INTO EGYPT

They are here, the two of them:

Abram, a hunched ox,
mule-strong, staggers away
from the palms shedding
their leaves in great weightless wings.

Already an old man,
visions, coarse as bees,
enter his nostrils, ears,
the places between his teeth.

With his right hand,
he motions to the girl –
she lifts her robe as she runs
her red veil fluttering in her face.

Sa'rai.

Her blue-black hair falls
in torrents down her back.
Her father's words are a bell,
their clapper a tongue:
To Abram you are given.

About that, she could not prophesy
as she did the births of ewes,
the dying of wells, the infestation of snakes.

➤

Nor did she foresee,
as they entered Egypt, the prince – brown as wetted
  earth –
nor his necklace of coral
nor the linen breathing in the doorway.

SA'RAI IN EGYPT

I am fourteen when Abram tells me I am beautiful.
There is no compliment in it, only a weighing,

as he does the skins of wine, the sacks of grain.
In the day, my mouth is always slightly

open. I have a habit of licking my lips, tasting salt.
While braiding my hair, I cannot let go.

I pull my hands through its weave
again and again... Even against

the potter's stone wheel, as it spins, I scrape
my hands. If I can touch, I can feel

the voice of things, leaking like sap,
tangible as resin.

In me, desire is viscous
as honey, willing itself to shape.

My gods have faces I can savor,
thumbs, thighs, genitals; I am green

with caresses. Then, Abram leaves me
at a door etched in black,

with an old woman
pouring water over the white marble floor,

and the music of a flute, each note naked, crimson,
pure.

SA'RAI AND PHARAOH

Here, far away from famine,
water is spilled

like transparent silk
over edges,

into the white mouths
of lilies.

Torches lengthen
from pale walls.

The pulse of her wrist
rings

like the bells
of camels.

She breathes.
He breathes.

The sun dips
amber,

rinsing
their bodies gold.

Her purpose
is clear.

He does not
know how he knows,

only
it wills him back

and back again,
circling.

PERHAPS

Let's suppose:
At first, for both, it was like a pear
cut in half. The muscle of the fruit,
the soft insides, tasted. Perhaps they swallowed.

Perhaps she was eager, being young.
And the musk of her newness was a wick
kindling against reason; his full mouth
working at a word.

Perhaps she danced: the roofs of the city lifting,
the sky unhinged, emptying into the Nile –
which at first resists, then succumbs,
then floods to its source.

Who then, would write their secret
when finally he gave her back,
undone?

SHAGARA TYUR MAITIN –
A TREE OF DEAD BIRDS

I am Sa'rai – the one who hears
the off-rhythm of bells, the ululation of war rising
into sky.

There is fire, and carcasses of bees.
I am parched, my lip split open.

I have rubbed at the dry, flat
flesh of stone; promise pulling at my breasts.

Fragrant, in veils and coins, Ha'gar
is brought, shimmering green, gold, turquoise, red;

a brilliant cloth bartered for wheat; a gift –
a child for Sa'rai.

I hear her girl's voice:
It is the Nile leaking from her throat.

To me will belong her long neck,
her nervous hands plucking at my rings,

her small arched foot, upon which I must
mark the blue stain, *slave.*

Thorn trees are here, so green their color warps.
Inside, the brittle spikes. Wild birds of the desert

➤

aim for its leaves; then screech, impaled.
Once I saw an owl,

its beak imbedded in its own heart,
trying to break free.

HA'GAR SEES SA'RAI

She's jealous, that's what everyone says.

Oh, she smiles at me, offers me things:
"Ha'gar, taste this bit of lamb...
"Ha'gar, use lemons to sweeten your breath...
"Ha'gar, let me soak your feet in rosemary..."
She goes on and on; you'd think she was my mother.
But I see her glancing at my beauty, my skin
the color of cinnamon, my coiled hair, my eyes –
nothing escapes her sight.

She can't stand to see me go to him, *her husband,*
    Abram.
Me, eleven years old, already a woman.
Last night she wept as she platted my hair,
stroked mallika oil on my limbs – I glistened like water.
My scent "filled the canopy with offerings."

Look at me: my breasts like figs, my nipples rosy
    with henna,
and on my belly – in all my secret places – the musk
    of cloves.

Sa'rai even wraps me in her own shimmering
robe. Her hands shake as she does this, so I know
she's jealous; she tells me over and over,
"Ha'gar, I do this because I must." As if I cared,
as if I weren't the important one, the one *he* wanted to
    bear his son.

➤

And so what if he is old, and tastes of ashes; so what if
his beard scrapes my cheek, or his wrinkled hands pull
at me?
I am the prize, am I not? He cannot get enough of me –
he is my first.

Why does Sa'rai worry so? She can do anything:
grow seed upon the rocks,
sow wild corn between the shadows,
cast the stones – she has the Sight.

But I see her – her hair the color of rain,
how she cries out in the morning,
her throat lifted as if for sacrifice.

THE JEALOUSY OF SA'RAI

Wasps, black and fat,
fill my head.
Restless,
I walk for miles.
Beneath my veil
my fingers scratch and scratch
at visions:
his wrinkled thighs
her inexperienced hands.
All around me
the women speak
their voices sift between my fingers

the desert uncoils in hot whispers,
snakes rise, tongue the air.
I hold my palms against my ears.
How could he
not love her?

The wadi fills with fleas,
with dung.
I cannot escape the scent.

Stuffed with duty, I shuffle to each place;
stagger under the measure of hours.

"You can bear this," Abram says.

➤

All around me, husks of seed,
desolate as scars.
I disrobe, shake silver
bracelets from my arms.
There the cooking fires,
there the cool knife for the lamb;
here the broken edge
of the bowl – sharp, needful.

I open the vein –
but no god comes
to me.

THE SACRIFICE

Look! He cuts the flesh of sacrifice.
Blood gushes down the gutters.
The white beast stumbles, kneels and dies. Abram
is thanking his God, the one who is plain as a thorn.

(Abram will have a son!)

He offers me – Ha'gar – first slice.

But I would rather steal this gift –
its weight in my hands –
hide in my tent, stuff my mouth,
swallow quick,
satisfy all desire in its rough taste.

In my tent I bury stolen things:
the shell knife Abram bartered for rope...
Sa'rai's bracelet, the thin one, of silver...
her topaz comb. They are mine. I cover them
with dirt; I empty my waste upon the mound.

(Abram will have his son.)

The women will fatten me, allow me anything.
I will enter their circle. They will weave cowrie shells
        into my hair,
wind red thread around my belly, paint horns
upon my breasts. They will cry out in jubilation.

Sa'rai will be silent; I will not speak.

HA'GAR'S BIRTHING

I am empty. Outside, the moon brightens.
Through the open flap of the tent,

I hear the occasional cry of an owl.
Far off, among the dunes, a woman's
laughter. My battle's waged.

My voice scrapes inside my throat.
Sticky, the blood between my legs.

I was the fire
in which the meat is seared;
the ember, blazing;
the bottom of a blackened pot.

I broke.

Crying out, I arched against my breaking.
But I did not falter. If there was a place
to hide, to steal away,
I could not find it.

This is what women know: We inhabit ourselves.
We are used – but also shape ourselves to use.

Sa'rai, those mornings when you slapped
the dough into loaves, your longing
pressing through your palms,
I'd walk past you,

my hands smoothing my belly.
Cruelty's in the small gesture. My smile.

The gully fills with moonlight. The sand
drifts, revealing pathways. My old angers rise
transparent;
the steam of soup, its odor gone.

Only this remains:
his small damp head,
his mouth at my breast,
his tiny hand.

Forgive me Sa'rai.

THE CHOICE

Sa'rai is dreaming her child:
a smooth boy, drifting in her body, silver as a leaf.

She is old – so old she hears the world cracking.
Light pushes out, and the dark strains to take.

The lavender sky folds back to blue evening;
the desert throbs inside its curves.

She falls, or is pushed, palms to the sand.
Her faith has dwindled to this falling, to the small

cry she releases daily into the heat.
Her face flickers, her long hair flares into shadow.

Inside the inside of her dream, she sees ruin:
smooth stones piling to an altar, lamp oil pouring black

tears against the gray slate,
the yolk of sun spilling orange.

She rises, moves her red palms across the air,
her bracelets' chime swallowed by the sand.

The shimmer, the salt, the sweat – a kind of man
stands before her, opening and opening:

You will bear child, Sarah.

He has given her a new name. The dunes shift,
the moon rises and rises; Sa'rai whispers

no...

HA'GAR CAST OUT

This is as near to faith as I can come:
this body

flawed and holy.

I did not know! I was mute
in the vast aftermath
when between my thighs
I pushed
a great blinding pain
an insight out of me
large
as a world.

I no longer trust vision.
Flesh transforms to muscle,
sinew, bone,
the rush of blood in the head,
the heel of the womb.

I offer it all –
my stink and smell,
my face, wearing away
against the bright day.
I am not lost.

Do you know
the rain in desert?
It comes hard, slapping
the face of sand; I hear
only the filling,
only the emptying.

THE SACRIFICE OF SARAH

What did he hope for,
when he dove into the damp

cavern of her body? *A son,* he said.
I swear, I thought he would refuse. But he took

his pleasure, opened himself into her.
And, after, he wiped her lush color from his palms,

lifted his hands to his face, as if to smell what had
been crushed.
Even so, her scent, ripe as desert jasmine, drifted
towards me.

Tell me: What God bled him, till in his eyes, I saw
a whole generation
crumbled into soot? The shale of a million lives
burning

inside the oven of his gray, gray eyes? Or was it I
who set it all in motion, obedient to the last,

when he cast away all I loved, or laid his son upon the
altar stone?
I lay out my questions like a shroud. What is sacrifice

if not that all is taken from you? Each part you love,
revere, whatever you count on, or hold close,

loosened, till the hollow of your chest becomes a
ringing bell,
and you are nothing but the air in which the clapper
tolls.

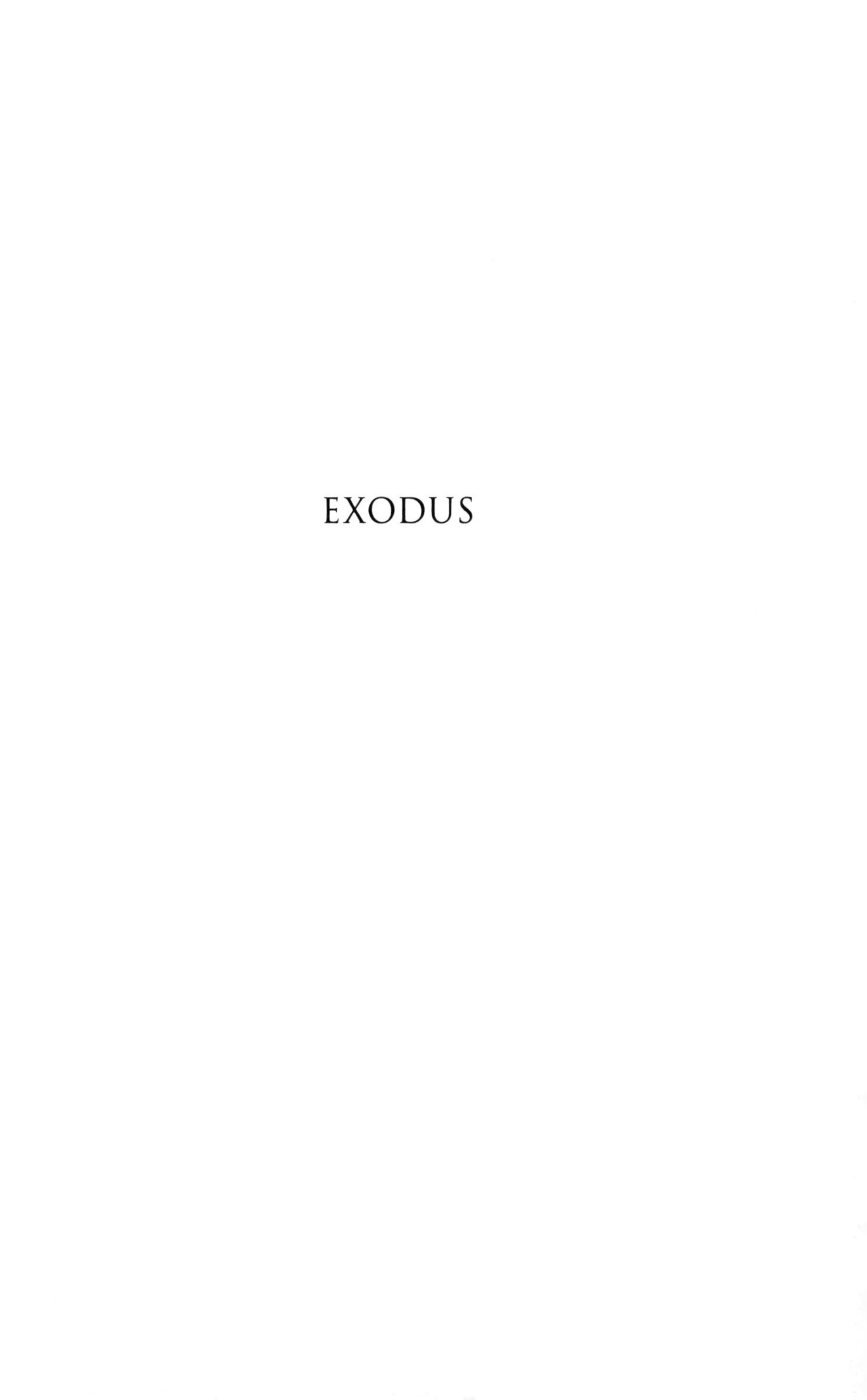

EXODUS

HUSH

Hush little baby don't say a word

He sang to me
his voice cracking
like the old battered couch out on the porch
facing the rusty yard
neighbors still burning coal
smudging the morning sky.

Hush little baby

Told me
about the Moses
he knew as a child
old man, white beard
who cured molasses in barrels in his barn.
The Klansmen came
and burned his barn
and him.
All over the county
people could smell that sweet
sweet molasses, burning
the whole night long.

Hush little baby don't say a word

➤

Cradled in his dark arms
I saw his streaked face
jaw grinding silent
his calloused hands
his pink nails, his dusty foot.

Papa's gonna buy you a mockin' bird

SALE

The yolk of my soul broke
when that auction man came near
and tasted my sweat:
The nigger wench is clean! he said.

There is the moment when you know:
you are broken. When he
licked me, his tongue,
like a huge finger, cracked me open,

tore out the soft meat,
filled me with sand.

Now I walk these dunes as if I were born to them;
and the silence – inside – dense as stone.

BELL

Sarah is dressing.
She is gathering her silk, her lace, her ribbons,
layer upon layer, till she is
the center of a bell,

the tongue inside
the inverted cup
of lace and ribbons and silk.
She is preparing.

She enters the dining room,
fumbling with the latch;
the foam of her dress
sweeps the floor, a whisper of silk.

There is nothing like
this sound, this kind of whisper.
She lifts her eyes to his face.
He is seated at the end of the dark mahogany table.

His eyes are gray flint;
they flick at her face, her breasts, skirt,
and suddenly, flare –
behind her – where

Harriet stands, head down.
Sarah has seen. She too casts her eyes
down, glances to see – if there is blood
on her soft gown.

She sits very still at the table.
Her bones will
snap, she is sure, if she moves too quickly
inside the bell of her dress.

UNTHINKABLE

In his mind he fastens upon the possible
circumference of Harriet's hair if undone
from its blue wrap, and then unbraided;
thinks of it like one might think of
a circle of light from a lamp, reversed.
In his imagining, her African hair opens,
a black spill upon his starched
pillow.

Then, as evening's blue descends,
he reconceives her face,
closed as marble,
its high plains, moisture
of the day trailing its way
down the glossy fact
of her jaw – to the impossibility
of her mouth – so compelling, even
the rippling scars she's cut upon her cheeks
do nothing to deter
his thought

that he might enter
beneath her ebony –
and her face, like her hair,
would reveal its purple tint,
till now unripened and unrisen.

SEASONING

I wake each morning,
no caught in my mouth –
a jaw-breaking shell
I crack with my teeth,
splinter into
the thousand *nos* of my days.
In the heat of my will
I cultivate its seed
till its scab
splits open, a bitter-sweet juice
on my tongue –
then, when evening comes,
I swallow it once again.

MASTER

He renamed her.

That was the sum of it. He was the apex
of a triangle, fixed, positional as a star.

He had done his calculations. Yet,
day by day, he grew leaner.

He determined
she was free

only to surrender. No
deviation from the norm. *No*. But

he was starving.
He weighed her refusal.

He was becoming skeletal. He could not
swallow. *No*
forced its way between his jaws,

its small teeth
gnawing at his throat.
He was a doctor. He would cure this.
He would close the doors, shut the windows,

measure the floor space. He would
pace the exact feet it took to cross
the room and back: Ten times
times ten times, times ten times,
circling smaller and smaller he would stand against her

no

WHIP

He removes his shirt.
Folds it over the fence.
The post is in the exact center
of the yard.

Harriet is bound –
Stripped –

shoulders,
back,
waist.

Sarah is at the window,
(No!) at the door; she flutters
from opening to opening:

This is the one he desired.
I know
he is willing
to break a body.

The woven leather whip
is as long as Sarah's own braid.
He balances its give and take,

weighs it in his palm, like a father
weighing a newborn;
calculates the geometry of the arc,
snaps tip to flesh.

He cuts,
measuring
seven lashes, then seven more
in the hot Sunday sun.

Sarah understands:
There is a kind of truth in this:

her watching –
his pause at each thrust –

Harriet's "Mercy!"

SUNDAY – SARAH

All is milky. The scraped sky,
my breath on the window,
the swell of my belly – though,
like frost beneath immaculate snow,
it hints of blue.

There is more to this world than what I know.

There are tulips, purple
as bruises,
fat bulbs sneaking upward
at first warmth.

I remember
that clear day, eight months ago:

I knew the promise of cool morning
would open into heat.

I knew – what I saw –
my palms pressed against
the glass – how she cried out only once –
"Mercy!"
Only that.

After, for the last time, he came to me –
laid his scourge upon my bed; and yet,
I shook my long hair loose –
and against his urgent press – his palm

across my breast – his breath –
my rooted tongue.

But soon, I know, it will be she
who lifts me to my woman's bed, reaches
into my woman's place, and
pulls his son from me.

COTTON

We move like a dark rain
among the white wealth of blossoms;
a tide, moaning
and bending between the rows –
between the call and answer,
the susurration of burlap sacks.

Peach brown, oxblood,
imperial yellow, mirror-black,
our hands are clots of color;
they are like mouths, opening, closing,
tearing the white
sprays of cotton.

The cotton is light as sea foam,
bright as the lost horizon.
And we – we are the black ships
come to port, to pick, and take,
breaking the white waves
in our wake.

THE MIRROR

In the big, immaculate house,
in a corner bedroom, his ironed white shirts,
still and stiff, glow faintly from the closet.

Sarah thinks of his cigar.
Its red round ash, like a small mouth
hot and whispering; how in the morning

he eats the soft egg from its shell.
She feels again his thin lips
across her face; his kiss.

She touches the edge of the white windowsill,
opens the tan leather book, fingers the soft
ribbon which divides it – runs her fingertip

inside the pewter bowl. In her palms,
she cups her breasts. They are small and pink.
She has never realized – her own body, naked in
    a mirror,

never thought of it till now –
the green throat of the sea,
its lips of white foam,

telling.

HARRIET LISTENS

Outside, the morning's sweeping rain.
We lie, not speaking, listening to its sound.
Her bedroom lifts out beyond the house – as if it were
    a ship.
Sarah rests upon her huge bed, plumed as a sail –
I on my mat – an anchor at its feet.

She is now in her ninth month – wide, rich, round –
like the oh she lets escape at daylight's end.
Her own pride brought me to her room.
Deep in night, she peers into my face, I know.

But this morning we lie silent – she does not call.
The rain outside drenches the trees; it wets
the green, the red, makes a curtain of yellow.
It is as if we are severed from the greater House –
    the land –
the life we know. She in her quilts; I in my cotton.

I do not speak at all – refusing, as I can nothing else.
But I listen for her call; none comes.
So it comes to me: this is a kind of speech –
this piling silence, this agreeing not to say.

This child in her – his – I had thought, months ago,
    to kill.
I gathered in the rue, the seeds and roots of cotton,
some tansey, pennyroyal, the cedar spirit –
mixed as I had been taught – as I had done
to me – three times before.

I argued – so deep was my pain – my own son
sent away; how all my people – in their blanched
    shame –
fear to have a son; tremble for their daughters.

So I thought: Should I grind with mortar those seeds,
those flower roots; make her a tea
to bleed her quickening out?
Why should she bear what I could not?

I stayed my hand – not for her,
no, nor any of her kind. Not for the gods
I left so far behind – not even for my own ripping sore.
    No.
Only because I could.

Now she is full, almost to her end;
Does she think, as I do,
about her plenty coiled within her womb; mine,
    sold away?
How it will be I who will help her to her woman's bed;
I who will stand strong between her legs; I who will pry
    his siring out?

SARAH AWAKE

The moon slants through the window.
There is no breeze. The baby whimpers in his cradle.
Harriet sleeps.

The edge of the bed is a cliff I lean over;
I fear the pull of falling. There's no haven here.

With only the candle, the room seems circular, as if it
were a cave.
We three, together – son, slave, mother – I discover,
family.
My ghosts keep knocking.

My mother's voice – *do not marry* – my father's
command,
the husband I was given. How easily I surrendered.

That night of whipping and conceiving – how easily
I loosened,
like rain, my hair. Did I love him, then? I wanted a son.
My corset of lies, now undone.

When he held my hand at wedding day, I saw,
in my mind's eye, a huge door close; I wonder,

was I not also bought in some small way? An offering
for land, prestige, manly honor kept?
Still, he prefers the one who sleeps here now. Still.

The way out? The path the moon makes.
My thoughts are dire, as if I were a child lost upon the marsh.

Flickering lights draw me on. Out there lies a great bog.
An owl calls. No one would help. The slaves cannot.
Am I to steal my son?

Harriet would flee alone –
ah, how fiercely he would follow.

The baby cries. My milk stains my blouse. I go to nurse.
Even in this, I transgress. Harriet wakes. Rises to her
prayer. Her arms expose her scars, like stars.

HARRIET SPEAKS

My words are clots of blood.
Their iron salt inside my head.
To her, I said *I will*

and to the boy, *Sleep now.*
My throat is open.
I taste the words: Shall I be released? I pray.
Longing can cause ruin.

Hope is taken, then baled like cotton.
To slake my need – I shake my yearning
like a dog does water. I've used my silence as a twine,
to wrap my soul inside.

Freedom is no simple thing; *Release me and I'll go.*
I pass through speech – carry slavery with me.
Sarah's sold her rings, her earrings made of pearl.
She seeks what else to sell – I fear her gaze will turn
to me.

Judgment comes if we endure – so the preachers say.
I speak into a rain drum, it fills with echoes.
Candles glow about the room. Am I now afraid
of silence – its rustle and great whisper,

the forest's ticking, the night and its huge shutter?
She and I designed our masks – for three –
mistress, slave, young master – yet I fear – after,
will she take these masks as real?

This leaving's like a breech,
a birth not turning. I light the pine,
I fan across this chasm. My whipping scars make
        a pattern:
map, mountain, star.

My words splatter – like rain after dust –
everything matters – we've named the boy:
        Sweet Laughter.
My soul leaps in and out of me – pulls its knife.
Summer will not return to ice, the broom

does not go back to straw. A great ship comes –
the ocean returns its bones; but there is only one
muddy road – and no stranger passes.
The moon will not pare itself to dark –

We will not go back.

MASTER II

He stares through the window
palms against the glass.
Inside this immaculate house
everything his sight touches – cracks
fault
lines stalk unseen inner breaks
shadows crumble
into ash
the long mahogany table flaws into
splinters
the window shatters inside
its pane.

Outside, the fog shifts.
Two figures, three, merge – disappear/appear/
dim/brighten/become obscure…
An upended tree fingers the air.

His lungs fill.

He should call out. Saddle a horse. Follow.
He should call out – call out, to his son…
Where are you? Why are you going?

CODA

WELL IN SAND

The Wonder Wheel is stopped.
The wind throws itself against its great rib,

but it does not move, only shudders a little
against the cold. Here in Coney Island,

two ancient women watch the storm
recede. They marvel at the ordinary sand, the
common water,

the plain wooden bench. Hattie and Sadie.
As bent as iron nails might be – with brand,
tattoo, scar.

Which arm is their own, they forget, sharing
the fluency of dream, their blurred, indigo speech.

Long ago, their silence dug a well in sand,
their words pinging into the water,
fresh as anything newborn.

At the bottom was a trembling,
an unseen disturbance –
the weight of self swimming towards self.

Runaways, they saved everything they could:
an infant, their torrential will, the cure for god.

➤

Inside the void they carved a labyrinth –
Inside that, they raised up Sweet Laughter.

Now Hattie's hair is light and bright as cotton in
the boll.
Sadie's coils in crown above her head.
Seeds of all kinds knot and sprout in the waves of
their hair.

They pivot like wheels over the sand; spin
into circles and spirals. Reality pools, iridescent, at
their feet.
In them, moisture and desert combine.

In them, everything is holy – everything profane.

CONEY ISLAND

I pace between two beaches –
Walk the wet, flat sand,
Leave no track.

If I push, just a little, the skin of this world will tear,
And I will enter another – forgetting this one.

But this raucous place,
Its great wheel peeling and flaking,

Its cooking smells, the splatter of fat,
The children splashing laughter back to the sea –
Oh Mother, how hard it is
To let it go.

Sticky – this living;
I've smeared my fingers
Eating at it like buttered corn.

Even the evening clings,
A delicate shawl of darkening blue.
My body – its spun flesh – trespasses,
Needing – still –
The ancient spell – of touch.

GOING THE DISTANCE

At the long bar of smoke
and dark whiskey, voices grind
into splinters.

Men who build their lives on steel, on rubber,
on things and the making of things,
line the bar, huge as boulders,

a Stonehenge of backs, necks, forearms,
knuckles roughened raw,
the wide palms of work. Out of the rock
of bodies, their man talk, the slow turn of shoulder,

I suddenly know –
That one.

I know my worn woman's body –
how it would fit to the center of him –
how I could travel from this cold harbor
to the light, which only I can see,

that would drench the dry weariness
I carry like a sponge. And for that, yes
I would go the distance, allow my flesh to become
a soft drum, a refuge

he could destroy –
I would tow his body down and down
into my sheer well of grief, salvage us
from fault, mistrust, the hunger

he could never name, or allow me to name;
but I would allow, for just that moment
when he lies spent, open as an opulent shell,
and I see myself in him –

a soft wailing
eased from its casing of stone.

CONEY ISLAND PRAISE SONG

In pale early morning, I stumble along the damp
 boardwalk.
I'm inside myself, as if blind, hands outstretched,
 feeling at the wet air.
I've stepped into Sight – I'm caught in its net.
My dreams are salt between my teeth.

The dolphins sing like bells, like chimes, their
 tinkling bliss.
I hear them as if I were aboard a ship, rocking. I hear
 the creak
of wood, the ancient sail; their song calls up my
 broken dead.

For so long, I have held the rosary of their bones,
 bleached and holy.
Now I open my hand to find only lines. I've shed
 my scars,
one by one, like notes, like letters – thin wafers
 of prayer
I can taste upon my tongue.

It is ecstasy to laugh, let go my measured heart,
to see the dolphins rise, orchids beneath their lids.
In their mouth is infant light – and within their
 ornate sound
my dead sing Praise Songs now.

OUT OF THE RUINS

The world turns over its dark rubble.
Cast the stones. I can read them.

Here. I do not forget.
In my sweat the old gods
glimmer.

Long ago
I lived as a stranger – the tilt of the world, pulling.

I have told my story slowly – leaving room for error;
a mosaic, fragments
of imperfection.

ACKNOWLEDGMENTS AND THANKS

The following poems have been published in *Rattapallax*, some in slightly different form: *A Bell Buried Deep,* Vol. 4; *Going the Distance,* Vol. 5; *The Sacrifice of Sarah,* Vol. 6; *Cotton,* Vol. 7; *Coney Island* and *Mami Wata,* Vol. 10.

Going the Distance has also been published in *BigCityLit.com.*

Ha'gar Sees Sa'rai, A Tree of Dead Birds, and *Sar'ai in Egypt* appeared in *Bridges: A Journal for Jewish Feminists and Their Friends,* Winter 2003.

A Tree of Dead Birds has also been published in *Natural Bridges*, March 2003.

* * *

I wish to especially thank George Dickerson, mentor and friend, for his generosity and brilliance.

And thanks to:

Barbara Aziz, Chris Brandt, Patricia Carlin, Michael Carmen, Ellen Cattalinatto, Enid Dame, Nawal El-Sadaawi, Sara Glover, Ritu Kalra, Kate Light, Rabbi Ellen Lippmann, DH Melhem, Jelayne Miles, Martin Mitchell, Alicia Ostriker, Angelo Verga, Judith Warner, The Sarah Lawrence Summer Writing Program.

NOTES

KORÉ, *page 3*

Earliest designation of the World Shakti or female spirit of the universe. Variations include Ker, Car, Q're, Cara, Kher, Ceres, Core. Reflection in the pupil of an eye was known as the Kore or "Maiden" in the eye. To the Arabs, it was the "baby" in the eye. The Bible calls either a daughter or the soul "the apple of thine eye" (Proverbs 7:2). (The Woman's Encyclopedia of Myths and Secrets, Barbara G Walker).

MAMI WATA, *page 4*

West African goddess of the sea, she is a mermaid with a complex personality. Exceptionally beautiful women who will have sex for money are called "mami watas." Her colors are red and white. *Uwa mmadu* means "the world of human beings," and *ndi mmadu* means "human beings."

SHAGARA TYUIR MAITIN – A TREE OF DEAD BIRDS, *page 17*

This phrase comes from *The Names of Things* by Susan Brind Morrow, Riverhead Books, 1997.

SEASONING, *page 41*

"Seasoning" was the term slave owners gave to the "breaking" of a captured African into slavery.

THE BIBLICAL STORY OF SARAH AND HA'GAR (EXCERPTED)

From Genesis, King James Version

The name of Abram's wife was Sa'rai. *11:29.*

But Sa'rai was barren; she had no child. *11:30.*

...and they came to Ha'ran and dwelt there. *11:31.*

Now the Lord had said unto Abram, Get thee out of thy country...Abram was seventy and five years old when he departed out of Ha'ran. *12:1; 4.*

...and they went forth to go into the land of Canaan. *12:5.*

And the Lord appeared unto Abram and said, Unto thy seed will I give this land: and there he builded he an altar unto the Lord who appeared unto him. *12:7.*

And there was a famine in the land: and Abram went down into Egypt...when he was come near...he said unto his Sa'rai, his wife, Behold now, I know that thou are a fair woman to look upon:...when the Egyptians shall see thee that they shall say, This is his wife, and they will kill me, but they will save thee alive. Say, I pray thee, thou art my sister: that it may be well with me for my sake...And...when Abram was come into Egypt, the Egyptians beheld the woman that she was very fair...and the woman was taken into Pharaoh's house. And...(the Pharaoh) treated Abram well for her sake: and (gave him) sheep and oxen, and she-asses, and menservants, and maidservants, and...camels. (But) the Lord plagued Pharaoh...And Pharaoh called Abram and said, What is this that thou hast done unto me? Why didst thou not tell me that she was thy wife? Why sadist thou, She is my sister? so I (might) have taken her for my wife? now, therefore behold thy wife, take her, and go thy way. *12:10–19.*

And Abram went up out of Egypt, he and his wife, and all that he had...And Abram was very rich in cattle, in silver, and in gold. *13:1–2.*

Now Sa'rai, Abram's wife, bare him no children: and she had a handmaiden, an Egyptian, whose name was Ha'gar. And Sa'rai said unto Abram, Behold now, the Lord hath restrained me from bearing: I pray thee, go in unto my maid; it may be that I may obtain children by her. And Abram hearkened to the voice of Sa'rai. And Sa'rai, Abram's wife, took Ha'gar her maid, the Egyptian, after Abram had dwelt ten years in the land of Canaan, and gave her to her husband Abram to be his wife. And he went in unto Ha'gar, and she conceived: and when she saw that she had conceived, her mistress was despised in her eyes. And Sa'rai said unto Abram, My wrong be upon thee: I have given my maid unto thy bosom: and when she saw that she had conceived, I was despised in her eyes. But Abram said unto Sa'rai, Behold, they maid is in thy hand. And when Sa'rai dealt harshly with her, she fled from her face. And the angel...found her...by the fountain in the way to Shur. And he said, Ha'gar...whither wilt thou go? And she said, I flee from the face of my mistress,

Sa'rai. And the angel...said unto her, Behold thou are with child, and shalt bear a son, and shalt call his name Ish'ma-el: because the Lord has heard thy affliction... Thou God seest me...she said...And Ha'gar bare Abram a son: Ish'ma-el (when)...Abram was eighty and six years old. *16:1-7; 11; 13–15.*

And when Abram was ninety years old and nine...God said...neither shall thy name any more be called Abram, but ...Abraham; for a father of many nations have I made thee. *17:1; 5.*

And God said...thy wife, thou shall not call her name Sa'rai, but Sarah...And I will bless her, and give thee a son also of her...she shall be a mother of nations; kings of people shall be of her. Then Abraham fell upon his face and laughed...Shall a child be born onto him that is a hundred years old?...And shall Sarah bear? And Abraham said unto God, O that Ish'ma-el might live before thee! And God said, Sarah thy wife shall bear thee a son indeed; and thou shall call his name Isaac: and as for Ish'ma-el, I have heard thee: Behold, I have blessed him, and will make him fruitful, and multiply him exceedingly... *17:15–20.*

And the Lord visited Sarah...for Sarah conceived and bare Abraham a son in his old age...Isaac. And Abraham was a hundred years old, when his son Isaac was born utno him. And Sarah saw the son of Ha'gar the Egyptian...She said unto Abraham, Cast out this bondwoman and her son: for the son of this bond-woman shall not be heir with my son, even with Isaac. And Abraham rose up early in the morning, and took bread and a bottle of water, and gave it unto Ha'gar…and sent her away; and she departed, and wandered the wilderness of Be'er-she'-ba. And God heard (again) the voice of Ha'gar. *21:1–5; 9; 14:17.*

And it came to pass…that God said…to Abraham…Take now thy son, thine only son Isaac, whom thou lovest…and offer him there for burnt offering upon one of the mountains which I will tell thee of… *22:1–2.*

And Sarah died in Kir'jath-ar'ba: Hebron in the land of Canaan: And Abraham came to mourn for Sarah, and to weep for her. *23:2.*

ABOUT THE AUTHOR

Veronica Golos is a poet, writer, editor, and teacher. After completing *A Bell Buried Deep*, she was awarded a three-month artist's residency by the Wurlitzer Foundation in Taos, New Mexico. She is at work on a new collection of poems inspired by her sojourn there.

Ms. Golos has a published chapbook, *No Ordinary Women*. Her work is also included in the chapbook, *Against the Tide: 3Poets4Peace*.

Ms. Golos was the award-winning Artistic Director for Literary Programs at the 14th Street Y in New York City from 1999–2003. As a teaching artist, she has led writing workshops for Poets House, Poets & Writers, the 92nd Street Y, and has taught Master Classes for Makor.

Veronica Golos currently lives in New York City with her husband, actor and writer David Perez, and may be contacted at vgdp@aol.com.